WHO IS JESUS?

WHO IS JESUS?

BY JAKE MENTZEL

WARHORN MEDIA
BLOOMINGTON, INDIANA

WARHORN MEDIA
2401 S Endwright Rd.
Bloomington, Ind. 47403
WARHORNMEDIA.COM

ISBN-13: 978-1-940017-50-1 (paperback)
ISBN-13: 978-1-940017-51-8 (pdf)
ISBN-13: 978-1-940017-52-5 (EPUB)
ISBN-13: 978-1-940017-53-2 (Kindle)

Cover design by Ben Crum. Interior layout by Alex McNeilly. The text
is set in 11/14 pt Minion 3 a typeface designed by Robert Slimbach.

CONTENTS

The Most Important Question:

WHO DO YOU SAY I AM?

About two thousand years ago, a baby was born in a barn (or maybe a cave, actually) outside a little city called Bethlehem. His mother was a woman named Mary. Her husband was a man named Joseph. They were poor. And they were from a place nobody liked named Nazareth.

That boy grew up to be a man. He lived the first thirty years of his life in utter obscurity. Nobody knew a thing about him. Then one day, when the time was right, he began to teach and preach.

He was such a popular preacher that thousands of people flocked to him from all around. There were rumors that he had special powers—casting out demons, healing the sick, making the lame to walk and the blind to see.

The poor and the needy, the broken and despised, loved him—because he loved and cared for them when no one else would. Because he healed them. Because he touched their pain. Because he told them the truth. And because he stood up to the establishment that neglected and oppressed them.

Which meant the establishment hated and despised him. The rich and powerful mocked him. The religious elite sought to have him killed. He exposed their hypocrisy. He threatened their stranglehold on religious and political power—through simple love and truth-telling.

For three years Jesus ministered to people, proclaiming the gospel of a kingdom that was at hand, and calling everyone he met to repentance.

Then one Sunday he marched into Jerusalem with his rabble of followers proclaiming him king and laying palm branches before him. The leaders of the city spent the whole week plotting to kill him, and he spent the whole week putting them to shame.

On Thursday of that week, one of his best friends had had enough of the tension, and betrayed him. In the middle of the night Jesus faced a kangaroo court that quickly sentenced him to death on trumped-up charges.

By Friday morning he was abandoned by his friends and left to be tortured and hung from a cross, where he died. From there, he was buried and sealed in a tomb.

But what happened on Sunday—no matter where you're coming from, or what you believe—changed the world forever.

Every single Sunday from that Sunday two thousand years ago to this very day—from Jerusalem where it all went down, to a cornfield in Indiana on the opposite side of the globe on a previously uncharted, unknown continent—this man's followers gather to proclaim that on that day his grave was empty. And that it still is empty.

You can hate it. You can despise it. You can resent it. You can laugh at it. But you cannot deny that the world we live in has never been the same.

All of Western civilization is built on this fundamental claim: That Jesus Christ rose from the dead. And that he lives to this day. And that his kingdom must and shall fill the earth.

"The people who walked in darkness have seen a great light. Those who dwelt in a land of deep darkness, on them a light has dawned."[1]

The name of Jesus is everywhere. His influence is undeniable—in politics, art, music, philosophy, you name it. Go take an art history course. Go to a philharmonic concert. Research the development of Western political theory or philosophy. Pick *any* discipline and trace it to its roots, and along the way you will have to deal with Jesus.

Here in Evansville, Indiana, the community in which I live and minister, there are churches on every street corner. If you stopped someone at the local Fall Festival and asked them about Jesus, nearly everyone would have an idea or an opinion about who he is and why he came and what he did and whether he's still worth listening to.

Jesus is so influential that every American president still, to this day, has to pay lip service to him, whether that politician's name is Biden or Trump, Obama or Bush.

Jesus has changed the world.

The question is why. There have been other great preachers. Other charismatic speakers who could draw a crowd. Other revolutionaries who threatened their era's political or religious order. Other prophets. Other miracle workers. Other messiahs.

What was it about Jesus?

This is the most important question anyone can ask. It's a question every serious person *must* ask. It's a question Jesus himself asked of his followers:

"But who do you say that I am?"[2]

Who is Jesus, really? Why has he had such an impact on human history? What should we do in light of who he is?

This book offers five answers, taken straight from the pages of the Bible, presented as simply and directly as I'm able:

1. Jesus is God.
2. Jesus is Man.
3. Jesus is our Prophet.
4. Jesus is our Priest.
5. Jesus is our King.

My goal here is not to offer anything new, or to sound especially profound. The truth is profound enough in itself. I just want to be clear and easy to understand. It's my hope and prayer that you will consider each of these five answers carefully, and come to see Jesus for who he really is.

1

This Changes Everything:
JESUS IS GOD

You are the Christ, the Son of the living God.

—The Apostle Peter (Matthew 16:16)

One day, Jesus was walking with his disciples. Ordinary people had begun to ask questions. Religious leaders were coming to him and trying to test him. Everyone wanted to know who he really was and what he was doing.

Why?

Because this man was performing signs and wonders and miracles. And he was preaching and teaching in a way no one had ever heard. And yet . . . he was just an untrained carpenter from a backwater town called Nazareth.

Pick a place nearby that everyone in your city or town looks down on. My hometown of Evansville, Indiana, is on the Ohio River, so Evansville people like to look down on people from *across* the river. No one important is supposed to come from Henderson, Kentucky. Especially no one who hasn't been to college or seminary. Especially no one whose ordinary job is blue-collar.

But that's exactly who Jesus was. He was a carpenter from Nowheresville, Israel.

Jesus knew what the buzz was about. And by this time, he had been living with and teaching some of his closest disciples for a couple years. So he decided to put the question to them.

"Who do people say that I am?"[1]

It's a good question.

Who do people say Jesus is?

If you were to answer that question right now, if you were to go out on to the street and ask ten random people who Jesus is, how do you think they'd answer?

A good person?

A good moral teacher?

An example of how to live?

A prophet, maybe?

Do you know what the answer the disciples gave was?

"Some say John the Baptist, others say Elijah, and others Jeremiah or one of the prophets."[2]

Now those are amazing answers. Why?

Because all those people were *dead*. Some of them for thousands of years. John the Baptist had his head cut off. Elijah and Jeremiah were loooong gone.

And so what were Jesus' disciples saying?

The best explanation that ordinary people can come up with, Jesus, is that you stepped out of the pages of history. They think you must be some great man of old, some prophet, come back from the dead. They really don't have any answers. That's why there's a buzz. That's why people are coming to you.

In other words, Jesus was doing the kinds of things you and I have only ever heard stories about. No one had an explanation. No one had an answer. Somebody must have come back from the dead. That was the best anyone could come up with.

So Jesus asked the question again. But this time he put it differently—this time he wanted to know what his closest disciples thought:

"But who do you say that I am?"[3]

A disciple named Peter answered: "You are the Christ, the Son of the living God."[4]

Now, if you can believe it, that is an even more amazing answer than the people gave.

Stop and think about it for a second. What was Peter *actually* saying?

Some people say that you must be some kind of ancient prophet raised from the dead. They feel like you must have walked straight out of the Old Testament into modern times. But I know that they haven't begun to touch the truth. You aren't some prophet come back from the dead. That's crazy. It's crazy because it's way too normal. No, you're much more extraordinary than that. You're the Son of the living God.

Think about that. Can you imagine ever meeting someone, living and traveling with him for years, and coming to the conclusion . . . this person must be the Son of God?

What would it take?

Who, after their first couple years of marriage, takes a step back and looks at their husband or wife, and says, "Yep. That person is probably the pinnacle of divine perfection."

Anybody?

I mean, I bet you thought you were marrying someone pretty great when you were getting married. But *no one* gets through the first couple years of marriage with any illusions of perfection, right?

Okay, maybe you're single. Have you ever had roommates or siblings? Any of them perfect?

You get the idea, right?

This is something we all have to reckon with. Something we all must face. These men spent three years with Jesus. They went from city to city, town to town. They ate with him. They traveled with him. They lived their lives with him.

And they came away from *that* convinced Jesus was the Son of God. Which is to say, God himself.

And more than that, they carried that conviction from Jerusalem to the ends of the earth, and in most cases, to their graves. They were tortured and killed.

Martyred. Because they would not give up their belief that Jesus is God.

They were changed men. Men on fire.

Two Choices

Here's another question for you. If you were a good moral teacher and someone looked at you and said, "You're so great . . . you must be God," how would you respond?

How would you expect a good moral teacher to respond?

What would be an appropriate response?

"Get behind me, Satan," maybe.

But that's not how Jesus responded. He said something very different.

"Blessed are you Simon, son of Jonah, for flesh and blood has not revealed this to you, but my Father who is in heaven."[5]

In other words, Jesus doesn't say what you would expect someone who is *just* a good moral teacher to say. He says, "Yeah. You're right. You get it. I am God."

Now I bet I can get you to agree with this statement: A good moral teacher would never, under any circumstances, claim to be God or encourage his followers to believe he is God incarnate.

Unless it were true.

So, is it true?

Jesus has only left us two choices:

1. Either Jesus is an insane narcissist, a deeply immoral person who allowed people to believe he was God.
2. Or he is exactly who he claimed to be. He really is God.

That's it. No other options. No middle ground.

C. S. Lewis put it best:

> I am trying here to prevent anyone saying the really foolish thing that people often say about Him: "I'm ready to accept Jesus as a great moral teacher, but I don't accept His claim to be God." That is the one thing we must not say. A man who was merely a man and said the sort of things Jesus said would not be a great moral teacher. He would either be a lunatic—on a level with the man who says he is a poached egg—or else he would be the Devil of Hell. You must make your choice. Either this man was, and is, the Son of God: or else a madman or something worse. You can shut Him up for a fool, you can spit at Him and kill Him as a demon; or you can fall at His feet and call Him Lord and God. But let us not come with any patronising nonsense about His being a great human teacher. He has not left that open to us. He did not intend to.[6]

So we come back to the question. The question everyone must deal with.

What if Jesus was telling the truth? What if the disciples really were right? What if none of this is an accident? What if there's a reason that Jesus is still worshiped to this day, and it's not just some strange fluke of history?

What if there's a reason that even the most wicked men on the planet have to pay lip service to him—which, by the way, is what happens every time an evil politician claims to be a Christian. And one of my favorite things about that every time it happens, is remembering that it's a fulfillment of ancient prophecy, thousands of years in the making: "Because of the greatness of Your power Your enemies will give feigned obedience to You."[7]

What if Jesus really is God?

Well, that would change everything, wouldn't it?

It already *has*. It has changed the whole world. And it might just be time for you to catch up with it—before it's too late.

Let's talk more specifically about the things that Jesus being God changes. I've got five of them:

1. The Beginning
2. The Then
3. The Now
4. The Future
5. The You

For each one of these, I want to take a brief look at the whole scope of what the Bible says. So we're going to look at the whole Bible, including the Old Testament. Because Jesus is God. Which means Jesus is much bigger than just the story of the gospels.

How does Jesus being God change each one of these things? Let's start with . . .

The Beginning

I'm going to start a sentence for you. And I want you to try and finish it. No cheating.

"In the beginning . . ."

Maybe you were able to finish that sentence. Maybe you weren't. But if you were, and you finished it this way, "God created the heavens and the earth," you quoted the first sentence of the first verse in all of the Bible—Genesis 1:1.

But there's another way to finish that sentence. And it's in John 1:

> In the beginning was the Word, and the Word was with God, and the Word was God. He was in the beginning with God. All things were made through him, and without him was not any thing made that was made. In him was life, and the life was the light of men.[8]

When God created the heavens and the earth in Genesis, he did it by speaking it all into existence.

Ex nihilo, as the fancy theologians like to say. *Out of nothing,* I like to say, because I'm not some dead guy writing in another language. He spoke and it came to be.

In the beginning was the Word. That Word is Jesus. The eternal Word of God. Jesus was there in Genesis, shaping the world, forming the sun and the moon and the stars, designing the plants and the animals and giving them life. He is the Word that God spoke that brought life to the world.

So, the story of Jesus doesn't begin in the manger. It begins at the beginning of everything.

So that's the first thing that Jesus being God affects: the beginning. The second is ...

The Then

By "the then," I mean all of history up until now. Jesus has been present for all of it. He didn't help create the world and then wait behind the curtain for his big scene in Act Five.

He's been overseeing the course of human history with his Father. But he's also put in literal appearances. Call them cameos, if you like.

The Bible says that Jesus is the image of the invisible God.[9] No one has seen or can see God the Father except by seeing Jesus.[10] Which means whenever we see God in the Bible, we see Jesus.

What do I mean? Here are some examples you can

find in the Bible. Maybe you're familiar with some of them.

When God walked in the Garden in the cool of the day with Adam, Jesus walked in the Garden.[11] When God shut up the door of Noah's ark, Jesus shut the door of Noah's ark.[12] When Jacob wrestled with God, Jacob wrestled with Jesus.[13] When Moses spoke to the burning bush, he spoke to Jesus.[14] When Shadrach, Meshach, and Abednego were thrown into the fiery furnace and King Nebuchadnezzar saw a fourth person in there with them—someone who looked like a son of the gods—Nebuchadnezzar saw Jesus.[15] When Isaiah saw his vision, and saw one seated on a throne surrounded by seraphim who covered their faces and their feet and cried out, "Holy, Holy, Holy!" Isaiah saw Jesus.[16]

And when Jesus was born, Mary held God in her arms. When Jesus walked this earth, God's feet touched the ground. When he shook a man's hand, that man shook hands with God. When he spoke, what he said were the words of God—no matter how profound or how prosaic. Everything from "I am the bread of life" to "I am thirsty."

Jesus lived the life we lived. Which is to say, God lived the life we lived. We will talk about this more in the next chapter, but everything that happened in the New Testament matters, because God did that. Everyone Jesus touched was touched by God.

But let's move on.

The Now

If Jesus was God then, Jesus is still God now. Where is he? Why? What is he doing? We'll talk about this at greater length later, but let me answer that briefly right now.

Jesus is reigning on high in heaven. He is dealing with his enemies. He is spreading and building his kingdom in the world, though the world rages against him. And that is why we are here. Because the King has not stopped building his kingdom. And that has ramifications for the fourth thing . . .

The Future

If Jesus is God, Jesus is coming back to make all things right. Right now, he is making his enemies into his friends. One day, he will come and rid the world of every last enemy. And the last enemy is death.

Jesus is there in Genesis, creating the world. He's there through the story of the Bible, directing and interacting with the history of mankind. And he's there in Revelation, at the end of all things, bringing judgment and justice and peace.

Of course, the lynchpin of it all is the story in the gospels. When Jesus put on flesh. When he lived a perfect life as a man. When he died for our sins. And rose again from the dead.

But that brings us to number five . . .

The You

If Jesus is God, that changes everything. And that means everything changes for you. And for me.

We don't get to stay the same.

Are you the kind of person that calls yourself a Christian?

I grew up in a Christian home, but I had this moment in high school where I *really* became a Christian. I was suddenly evaluating *everything*. Everything in life that I thought would make me happy. Everything in life that I thought mattered. Everything I thought I was. That I found my identity in.

I was trying desperately to be honest with myself. To figure myself and the world out. I had been to some churchy things. I went to church growing up. I'd go to Young Life or whatever every once in a while.

But let's be real. Why did I go to Young Life? I went for the one thing that mattered most to me.

Girls.

But this was different, because life was hitting me differently. Sometimes life hits us in the face. God gives us wake-up calls. Suddenly things get real. Has that ever happened to you?

You get in a car wreck. You have a brush with death. You get arrested. You face jail time. You get sent to prison. It happened for a friend of mine who is now a pastor, when he got his then-girlfriend (now-wife) pregnant.

And then you have to decide. Am I going to wake up and face reality, or am I going to try to sleep through this and keep doing me?

I had a moment like that. It wasn't a big cathartic scary moment like a car wreck. It was kind of the opposite. For me, it was waking up and realizing that I had everything I had always worked for. The things I had always thought I wanted were within my grasp—sports, cute girlfriend, good grades, college scholarships. And it didn't make me happy. In fact, it all felt empty. Meaningless. A big bunch of nothing that couldn't possibly bear the weight of the big gaping wounds of my heart—wounds caused by my own sins and the sins of others against me.

I was left with a hunger and thirst for a happiness and purpose that nothing in this world could give me.

So I began to cry out to God. For real. Not fake. Not pretend. But for real.

And at some point, God led me to this realization. I realized that if God really is God, and if he is holy, and if he really made me and the world and everything in it, *that matters. That changes everything.* That changes how I live. That changes what I live for. That changes how I interact with everyone.

It was revolutionary. If God is God, his life doesn't revolve around me. My life has to revolve around him.

I found myself asking: Does God speak? He does? To us? Everything he has to say about why we're here? What's the point? What's the purpose? What's the meaning? How do I live? What do I live for? It's written down in a *book*?

I HAVE TO READ THAT BOOK. I HAVE TO READ IT AGAIN AND AGAIN AND AGAIN.

And so I did. And that was the beginning of God transforming my life. It was the beginning of what led to me planting a church in my hometown. It's what led to me writing this book.

I was just a guy who wanted to have a cute girlfriend and play some baseball and get a scholarship to a school where I could get a degree to earn some money and maybe, if I was lucky, make a difference somehow along the way—whatever that meant.

But Jesus changed everything.

I felt I had two choices before me. Stop calling myself a Christian, because that was a lie—I was a fraud, and the way I was living proved it. Or read the Bible, believe it, and obey it. All of it. For all of life.

I had to order my life around God and God's words. I had to really follow Jesus. Not pretend to follow Jesus, or merely say I followed Jesus. I couldn't get away with adding a little bit of spirituality to my life to feel better about myself. Not anymore.

I needed to get to church. Not for girls. But because I needed Jesus.

I had to stop paying lip service to God. Because he is God. He demands all of us.

And that's why he became a man. To give us all

of him. So that we could be his and he could be ours. That's why we gather on Sundays.

Jesus is God. And that changes everything.

2

In Every Way:
JESUS IS MAN

And she gave birth to her firstborn son and wrapped him in swaddling cloths and laid him in a manger, because there was no place for them in the inn.

—Luke 2:7

I moved my family down to Evansville to plant Church of the King in the summer of 2020. The timing was . . . special.

When we got down here, one of the things I'd hoped to do was find a good baseball team for my son to play for going into the fall. Lots of teams were having tryouts, and he had played shortstop for one of the better teams in the state of Indiana before we moved down from Bloomington. In my mind, the question was never *if* he would make a team. The question was *which* team we would end up *choosing* for him to play for.

As it turns out, the answer was none of them. We never got a choice, because he never got an opportunity. He was cut from every team he tried out for. And when spring came, he was cut from the recreational league all-star team. He was only allowed to play baseball at the lowest level possible—the level where you stand in right field picking dandelions and waiting for your free drink when the game ends.

How does a kid go from starting shortstop on an elite travel team to being relegated to rec league?

I was angry. And frustrated. And so was he. From my perspective, he clearly deserved to be treated better and evaluated higher. He wasn't being treated fairly or respected properly. Politics and relationships were taking precedence over what my son deserved. It was hard not to take it personally.

Of course, this story has a happy ending. My son eventually found his place on a good team. But it was a struggle to get there.

Here's my question. Is this a struggle that Jesus can relate to? Can I look at my son and say, "Son, Jesus knows what it's like to be rejected and treated unfairly"? Does God know what it's like for me to feel like my son was unfairly rejected?

This is a small, trivial, silly example, I know. Many people have experienced much worse, and no doubt felt more justified in thinking that Jesus can't understand what they're walking through. The world is full of tragedy, sin, and heartache. Children grow up in broken homes or with parents dead or in prison. Little boys and girls are harmed in the worst ways by the people they should be most able to trust. By the people God ordained to protect them.

But that's why I picked a silly, small, trivial example. Because as it turns out, nothing we experience in this life—not the big, sad, tragic things, or even the smallest, most trivial things—are things that Jesus can't relate to.

And that's because Jesus isn't only God. Jesus is also fully a man. But let's take a step back for a minute.

Picture Jesus

When you imagine Jesus being a man, what do you imagine? Do you have pictures and images of Jesus in your mind? Have you ever stopped to ask where they come from?

Maybe you grew up at a church that had pictures of Jesus in it. Or you had a grandma that had a painting of Jesus on the wall somewhere. Or you grew up with a story Bible. Or with *The Passion of the Christ* or *The Chosen.*

Isn't it kind of true that most of the images we have in our heads of Jesus look kind of more like bearded ladies with pretty hair and soft, glowing expressions than what we would recognize or respect in a man if we met him on the street?

At our church, if you have a baby, we give you a storybook Bible that has pictures of Jesus. It's the same storybook Bible we use in our nursery. But, just the same, I hate pictures of Jesus, even in the storybook Bibles we use at our church.

Why?

Because there's not one picture of Jesus that tells the whole truth about him. It's not possible. That's at least one of the reasons God forbids us to make images of him.

The reality is that every artist has a characterization of Jesus in their minds that is uniquely their own. That's what they are trying to show you with a picture. It's a Jesus made in the image of the artist.

And so you have images of soft, wussy Jesuses. Bearded ladies. Or really boyish Jesuses. Because I guess that's what most artists are nowadays.

And that's what gets stuck in our heads and our kids' heads and lodged in our cultural understanding of who Jesus is.

There are a few descriptions in Scripture of what Jesus looks like. One is in Isaiah, and it's actually a prophecy about what happened when Jesus died on the cross. Isaiah says he was so marred and disfigured that we couldn't stand to look at him.

Another description is from the book of Revelation, and it describes Jesus with a sword coming out of his mouth, with his robes drenched in blood, and with the words "King of kings and Lord of lords" written on his thigh like some kind of amazing tattoo.[1]

Why doesn't anyone draw pictures of *that* Jesus?

Because that Jesus isn't safe. That's why.

Everywhere you look, people are trying to take the edge off of Jesus. They're trying to make him safe.

Everyone wants to make Jesus *just a man*. Maybe a good man. But just a man. And more than that, a man in our own image. Or worse. Less than a man. A bearded lady.

But Jesus is not just another man. As we saw in the last chapter, no one has had a greater impact on the world than Jesus. No one. So Jesus demands to be taken seriously. Jesus is the Son of the living God. Always has been—from eternity past to this very moment. And that changes everything. That means we must order our lives around him.

Jesus and Superman

But there is a way to react to the world's kitschy, wussy Jesus that is also harmful. In our zeal to exalt Jesus as God, we can be guilty of downplaying the fact that Jesus is also a man. And, believe it or not, that's just as bad.

But it's the type of thing that each of us are guilty of doing all the time. Let me explain.

Have you ever felt like Jesus is not able to relate to you? Have you ever felt like he couldn't possibly understand what your life is like or the pain you feel? Have you ever felt abandoned by him? Have you ever felt alone, or like you can't come to him? Have you ever felt overwhelmed by anger or grief or sadness and felt like Jesus wouldn't get it?

If you answered yes to any of those questions, you've fallen into this trap.

It's really easy to do. It's really easy to have a Jesus that can only exist in stained-glass cathedrals. A Jesus who is *only* holy. Who is beyond us.

Sometimes in our minds, we're tempted to sort of think that Jesus cheated. That he was really only a fake man. Not a man-man. Not in the same way we are. He must've had it easier somehow.

We think he was a man the same way that Clark Kent was a man.

You know Clark Kent, right? Superman?

Does Clark Kent bleed?

No. Not really.

He can dress in a suit and wear dorky glasses, but at the end of the day, he's an alien from another planet. He is not actually like us. And no, in fact, he doesn't bleed. He's Superman. Bullets bounce off his chest. He can fly and shoot lasers out of his eyes and see through walls just as well in a three-piece suit as in a spandex onesie. Putting on glasses doesn't make him vulnerable to anything except being made fun of.

He's always Superman. He only pretends to be a normal dweeb like the rest of us so he can hang with his girl Lois. Which is some creepy alien behavior, if you ask me. But you didn't, so I'll move on.

My point is, that's how we sometimes think of Jesus.

He's God, except he pretended to be a man for a while or something. So he could hang out with us, I guess.

But he doesn't know what it's like to really be a man. To suffer. To bleed. To be lonely. Or even hungry. Did Jesus even need to eat?

That kind of thinking comes from the deceiver, and it is meant to take you, in your despair, in your suffering—because you've been abused and abandoned and betrayed and hurt—and to make you feel isolated from Jesus. Like you can't come to him. Like he is forever and always beyond your reach.

Or worse, it's meant to make you into a hypocrite.

Because if you think Jesus was faking it when he came and lived as a man, you'll think living the Christian life is just faking it. You'll think it means only *pretending* to be happy and holy. Pretending that your pain and your suffering and your sin isn't real. That your anger and your lust aren't really real.

Because you have a Jesus you can't bring them to. And you feel like you're not supposed to have them in the first place.

Do you know the type of Christian who lives in that sort of denial? Who pretends?

You might hear them say things like, "I never get angry!" And yet you feel like they're kind of sort of *always* angry. And that they just don't know how to be honest with themselves about it. That they're maybe even scared of what will happen if they are.

Here's why they're scared and pretending. They

can't take their anger to Jesus, because they have a Jesus who has never been angry. A Jesus who was never tempted. A Jesus who never suffered.

And so it's just as important for us to understand that Jesus is a man. In every possible way—physically, emotionally, and spiritually.

His life wasn't a game. His struggles weren't a show. And there is not a thing in your life that you have gone through, that you are going through, or that you will go through, that he cannot sympathize with you in. Everything from growing up without a mom or a dad to being rejected by the Little League baseball team.

Let me explain.

Physically

Did you notice the passage at the beginning of this chapter? It's the Christmas passage. Maybe you've memorized it. Maybe you remember Linus reciting it in that Charlie Brown Christmas movie that your parents put on when you were growing up. But here's what it tells us:

Jesus was born. Which means that Jesus lived in a woman's belly for nine months. And then he came out in the usual way. He was a baby. And as a baby, he did all the normal things babies do.

He was a boy with parents and friends and siblings. He went through puberty. He learned how to work. He was known as a carpenter and as the son of a carpenter. People were offended at his teaching, and what did they say? "Is not this the carpenter, the son of Mary, and brother of James and Joses and Judas and Simon?"[2]

We know this guy. He's just a carpenter. His mom is Mary. We know his brothers.

In Scripture we see Jesus being hungry. One of the funniest things in Scripture to me is this little verse in Matthew 4:2. It says that after fasting forty days, "he was hungry."

Duh. You mean after going forty days without food, the man was hungry? You don't say!

Why did something so obvious need to be said?

The answer is just as simple. Because we wouldn't believe it unless the Bible told us so.

Given the chance, we will make Jesus into Superman. The kind of Superman that can go forty days without food and not be hungry. So Scripture stoops to us and says, "Jesus was hungry."

He was also thirsty. He asked the woman at the well for a drink. Even when he was hanging on the cross, he was thirsty enough to ask for a drink.

So he was hungry, he was thirsty, and he got tired. And guess what we see in the Bible? We see him eating and drinking and sleeping. Like a hungry, thirsty, and tired person would.

I think one of Jesus' most relatable moments is when he is so tired he sleeps through a storm and his disciples have to wake him up because they're afraid the ship will sink. Or when he retreats and climbs a mountain just to get away from people to rest and pray and be by himself for a while.

Find those passages in the Bible some time. You'll notice they come after big crowd moments—like feeding five thousand people. Have you ever been in a big crowd for a while, and then just needed some alone time?

Jesus was human. He got to the end of a bunch of people time, with crowds asking for miracles, and he needed to get away and be alone and pray.

Just from a pure physical standpoint, if you've ever been that tired—that worn out—Jesus has been there.

Jesus knew hunger and thirst and pain and suffering and tiredness. Unlike Superman, Jesus could be cut. Jesus bled.

He also knew the joy of hard work and the pleasure of food and drink.

Emotionally

So Jesus has a body like us and relates to us physically. That's one thing. But maybe that's not where we tend to get tripped up. Maybe it's when it comes to his emotions.

But here's the thing. In the Bible, we see Jesus running the full gamut of emotions. He had the same kinds of relationships we have.

He loved his mom. He loved his friends. He loved children. Not just generally, like, *I love people in general.* Maybe you're like me and think it's easy to think of Jesus that way—that he just sort of loved everybody with an equal, vague, general, zen sort of love.

But Jesus loved people specially. Just like you love your mom or your dad and your siblings and friends differently than someone you've never met. For example, John was known as "the disciple Jesus loved."

And because Jesus loved people, that meant he also was sad. And wept. And grieved.

In John 11, Jesus was told this: "Lord, he whom you love is ill."[3]

They were talking about a man named Lazarus, who got sick, and eventually died. When Jesus learned about it, he cried. Just like you and I would.

Jesus also wept in other parts of the Bible too. He wept over the hardness of people's hearts, when they wouldn't turn from their sin and let Jesus care for them.

Jesus also had compassion for the poor and the sick and the needy.

And because he had compassion and love, he got angry.

He got angry, because the people of Israel made the temple of his heavenly Father into a den of thieves. He got so angry, he made a whip and chased people out of temple.

He got angry when they tried to keep the children

from coming to him: "He was indignant and said to them, 'Permit the children to come to me; do not hinder them; for the kingdom of God belongs to such as these.'"[4]

Maybe my favorite time Jesus got angry was also recorded in Mark. In that story, Jesus was teaching in the synagogue on the Sabbath, and there was a man there with a withered hand.

Jesus looked at the man with a withered hand and had compassion on him. He saw someone who needed to be healed. But instead of having compassion, some of the people there that day saw an opportunity to cause harm to Jesus. They were waiting to see if he would heal the man, so that they could accuse him of breaking God's command not to work on the Sabbath.

Think of how twisted this is. They were so intent on getting rid of Jesus that they were hoping he would perform a miracle and heal someone, just so that they had grounds to accuse him.

Jesus knew what was happening. So he looked around and called the man over, and asked everyone there a question.

"Is it lawful on the Sabbath to do good or to do harm, to save life or to kill?"[5]

Crickets. No one said a word.

And the Bible says this: "And he looked around at them with anger, grieved at their hardness of heart, and said to the man, 'Stretch out your hand.'"[6]

And right there, in that one story, you have anger and grief and defiance.

And that's the Jesus I love.

Isn't that the Jesus you love? The Jesus who stares down the crowd? The Jesus who calls their bluff? Who sees the weak and the needy and the vulnerable, and who moves toward them, no matter what it might cost him?

That's the Jesus I love, because that's the Jesus that moved toward me in my sin and weakness and need, at tremendous personal cost.

Jesus' enemies have always been like that too. Small and petty and shameless. To them, people don't matter. They're pawns in power games. But people are never pawns to Jesus.

There are a lot of other emotions you can find in Jesus. You can find humor in his teaching—especially in the ways he mocks the religious leaders of his time. The image of swallowing a camel is kinda funny, and that's what he says the religious leaders try to do with all their rules.[7] He also depicts hypocrites as the kind of people who walk around telling everyone about the tiny specks they have in their eyes, while they have giant logs sticking out of their own eyes.[8]

But you also find Jesus agonizing as he approached his death, pleading that the cup of God's wrath would pass from him.

You can find him lonely and betrayed, even by his closest friends and by his family.

It wasn't just Judas who betrayed him, remember. Everyone left him at some point. The Apostle John tells us, "Not even his brothers were believing in him."[9]

In other words, Jesus knows what it is to be abandoned. Betrayed. Alone. Not just by enemies out there somewhere, but by his closest family and friends.

He was beaten, slapped, spat on, mocked, stolen from, and lied about.

So physically—Jesus has been there. Emotionally—Jesus has been there.

How about spiritually?

Spiritually

If it's hard to believe Jesus can relate to us physically or emotionally, it's even harder to believe he can relate to us spiritually. And yet it's the place that maybe matters most.

On the one hand, it's easy to look and make some spiritual observations about Jesus. For example, Jesus prayed. If Jesus prayed, we should pray. Jesus worshiped the Father. He did the work of his Father. He said the words of his Father.

But what we have a hard time accepting and understanding is this part of Jesus' spirituality right here, from Hebrews 4:15: "For we do not have a high priest who is unable to sympathize with our weaknesses, but one who in every respect has been tempted as we are, yet without sin."

How is it possible to be tempted by sin . . . and not have sin? Every temptation that we face meets a sinful desire in us.

So we don't know how to think about Jesus being tempted. That's where we are most likely to think, "Well . . . he's just Clark Kent. He's not really like us. He wasn't *really* tempted."

But Jesus was tempted. In fact, Jesus was led into the wilderness and tempted by the devil himself. Jesus faced the same temptations Adam and Eve faced in the Garden of Eden. And that's not a coincidence.

You remember, Jesus was fasting in the wilderness. And the Bible pointed out that Jesus was hungry. Really hungry. And then the devil tempted him with forbidden food—"Turn these stones into bread."[10] He was also tempted to give himself to death. The serpent told Adam and Eve, "You will not surely die"—he told Jesus to throw himself off the temple, and trust that God would send his angels to save him. And Jesus was tempted to worship the devil in exchange for the kingdoms of the earth.

When the Bible says that Jesus was tempted in all ways as we are, in every respect as we are, it means *all ways.* It means *every respect.*

That doesn't mean that the temptations Jesus faced are identical to our own. He didn't live billions of lives. He lived one life.

But isn't there a difference between him and us?

Yes. One. And here it is. When we're tempted, evil

desire rises up in us to meet that temptation. And that's sin.

But when Jesus was tempted, there was no evil desire. He didn't sin, even in his heart. And that's why we can trust him with our temptations, even when we fall prey to them. Because he's been there in the fight. And he's won the fight. Every single time.

It's essential to understand this: there is nothing in your life, no temptation, no weakness, no suffering, that Jesus cannot look at and say, "I know what that's like."

He even knows what it's like to bear the weight of the consequences of sin. Not because he sinned. But because he bore our sins and their consequences for us. To the point of death. Even death on a cross.

Jesus has been there. Wherever you are. Wherever you've been. Jesus has been there before you. He can walk with you through it. And he can get you to the other side.

Putting It All Together

A couple days ago I was reading a blog post from a couple in our church who have walked through three miscarriages—one after the other after the other, during an already difficult time in their life.

Miscarriages aren't a thing that we talk about often, so we don't realize how common they are. But they are.

In his blog post, this father was writing about the grief and the anger and the bitterness and the sense of guilt that he has had to deal with. And the ways he still deals with and carries those things today.

It's hard. It was a sad post. But it was a post that ultimately was about the comfort we have in Jesus. And he quoted this little bit from a Charles Spurgeon sermon. Spurgeon was a nineteenth-century Baptist pastor from London, and he's a hero of mine. I named one of my sons after him.

Here's the quote:

> If in my grief I fled to Jesus, and there was about him a secret inability to sympathize, an incapacity to admit me to his heart; pure as crystal though that barrier might be, I should dash myself against it, and die in despair. A Jesus who never wept could never wipe away my tears. That were a grief I could not bear, if he could not have fellowship with me, and could not understand my woe.[11]

Jesus knows what it is to suffer. And to weep real tears, with real sadness. And that means he knows how to comfort those who suffer. Because he's been there. And it means he knows how to help those who are weak and tempted. Because he's been tempted in every way as we are, yet without sin.

Jesus is God. But Jesus is more. Jesus was out of our reach. But he's not anymore. Not because we can reach higher. But because he came down and got low, right down with us at our level.

Jesus became man. And in him infinite holiness meets with perfect meekness and humility. He is higher than the heavens, and he dwells with the broken, the needy, and the contrite of heart. Which means you can actually come to him.

When Jesus was born, Mary held God in her arms, because God became a baby.

When Jesus walked the earth, God's feet touched the ground, because God had feet.

When Jesus shook a man's hand, that man shook hands with God, because God had hands.

Jesus has a body like ours. That body was broken for our sins. Those hands and feet were pierced for our transgressions. And they still, to this day, bear those marks.

And that means you can come to Jesus with your burdens. Big and small. With your pain. With your sins. With your suffering. And you can find in him someone who understands. And is ready to forgive. To heal. And to restore.

It doesn't matter if you've been rejected by a Little League team or if you've been hurt deeply by someone very close to you. It doesn't matter if your sins are small, or so big that you're afraid to tell anyone because of what they might think. Jesus knows. Jesus understands. And you can come to him.

PART TWO

Between Two Worlds:

JESUS OUR MEDIATOR

For there is one God, and there is one mediator
between God and men, the man Christ Jesus.

—1 Timothy 2:5

So far we've said that Jesus isn't *just* a good person. Or *just* a good teacher. He didn't leave us the option of landing there.

Either he's a madman, or he is exactly who he said he is. He's God. And he is. And that changes everything.

But he became a man. A real man. Not in a pretend way, like Superman wearing Clark Kent glasses.

If you cut him, he bled. He lived a normal life. He was born like us. He was a kid like us. He grew up like us. He got hungry and thirsty and tired, like us. He ate and drank and slept, like us. He had a family with siblings and he worked with his hands and he suffered. Like us. He was lied about and betrayed and lonely. He was sad. He cried. He got angry. He loved his mom and his disciples and friends like Lazarus and he loved children.

And that means there's nothing in this life you can walk through—no pain, no suffering, no temptation—that he doesn't understand. That he can't relate to. That he can't say, "I've been there. I get it. I sympathize." And that's important. Because in Jesus, we have a God we can come to.

So Jesus is fully God. And fully man. Two natures united in one person. Jesus Christ.

Before we go any farther, I want to step back and ask the big question: Why. Why did the eternal Son of God have to take on flesh and become a man? Why did that happen? This chapter introduces us to the last three answers to our question, Who is Jesus?

Between Heaven and Earth

Here's a question for you to consider. If you were to look across the sweep of human history, and you could pull on a single, solitary thread that united all religions, what would that thread be?

I might put it like this. All religions across all times and places are man's attempt to bridge the gap between heaven and earth.

Here's the problem. Man is the one who divided heaven and earth in the first place.

First, we must understand that we were designed

by God to be the bond, the link between heaven and earth. When God made Adam and Even in the Garden, he made them to unite heaven and earth. Think about it.

On the one hand, you have God in his heaven, surrounded by angelic majesties. We don't know much about them, but we do know that they are spiritual beings who reside in the heavenly realms—they are unseen principalities and powers that have the ability to manifest themselves to us, but they are not of this earth.

On the other hand, you have the lower creation. Everything we see being created in Genesis. The plants and animals and birds of the air and fish of the sea. Whatever else you want to say about them, they are primarily physical beings. As opposed to spiritual.

What about us, though?

In Genesis 1:26–28, it says this:

Then God said, "Let us make man in our image, after our likeness. And let them have dominion over the fish of the sea and over the birds of the heavens and over the livestock and over all the earth and over every creeping thing that creeps on the earth."

So God created man in his own image,
in the image of God he created him;
male and female he created them.

And God blessed them. And God said to them, "Be

fruitful and multiply and fill the earth and subdue it, and have dominion over the fish of the sea and over the birds of the heavens and over every living thing that moves on the earth."

There's some debate among theologians about what it means to be made in God's image. Does it mean that we're sentient, moral, spiritual beings like the angels in heaven? Or does it have more to do with our place as authorities over God's creation, doing the work of governing and ruling in his place, as his imagers?

I don't want to get into the nuances of that discussion. What is indisputable is that man is unique above everything else in this world. And that man is, in fact, a moral, spiritual being in a way that dogs and cats are not, and in a way that the host of heaven is.

Later, in Genesis 2, we get a fuller picture of how God made man:

Then the LORD God formed the man of dust from the ground and breathed into his nostrils the breath of life, and the man became a living creature.[1]

There you have it. What makes man unique? We are both spiritual beings, and yet made of the dust of this earth. Heaven and earth are united in man.

In a very real sense, that makes our first parents, Adam and Eve, the first *mediators*. Not because there was a conflict or dispute—which is what you probably think of when you think of a mediator—but because we were positioned by God as a go-between between heaven and earth.

Adam was responsible to represent God before all of creation—both his character and his ways. This is what we call the work of a prophet. He was also responsible to represent all of creation before the court of heaven—the work of a priest. And he was to govern all of creation in God's place, filling the earth, subduing it, and extending God's good governance beyond the borders of Eden—the work of a king.

Adam, with Eve by his side, was the mediator between heaven and earth—as prophet, priest, and king—the pinnacle of God's creation. But all was not well.

The Great Divorce

Satan, a member of the host of heaven, and depicted in the Bible as the dragon, the great serpent, came to Eve, Adam's wife, and tempted her to rebel against God. We don't know a lot about why he chose to rebel against God and to lead our first parents in rebellion, and it's not wise to speculate. But we do know that he was arrogant, envious, and full of cunning. It's easy to imagine that he did not like the exalted position that Adam and Eve enjoyed in God's economy, and felt himself in every way our superior.

What we do know is that through his deception

of Eve, he convinced both Adam and Eve to disobey God and eat the forbidden fruit of the tree of the knowledge of good and evil.

When Adam did this, he handed his crown to Satan. And man fell from grace, from life, from his lofty position as God's mediator between heaven and earth. There was a great split. A great divide. Heaven and earth were divorced into two kingdoms, at war with one another.

Man was no longer fit to represent God to the world, or the world to God, because man handed the keys of the kingdom over to Satan, whom Scripture calls "the god of this world."[2]

What Adam and Eve did that day, they could not undo. What they lost, they could never get back. There was no going back to that original state. Sin entered the world. And from there, there was only death. And all of creation fell with Adam and is under God's curse. Thorns and thistles.

All of our religions are an attempt to bridge the gap we made between heaven and earth. But it is impossible. We cannot restore what we have broken.

But God had a plan and a purpose. One that he had designed before the foundation of the world. The day that Adam and Eve fell in the Garden, God promised that there would be a Savior, who would come and crush the head of the serpent and take back what was rightfully his.

And God began to work out his redemption in history, raising up men who were pictures of the Messiah, the Savior, the Mediator to come. Prophets. Priests. Kings. Some of them, all three at once—or close to being all three at once. Like Noah. And Abraham. And Job. And Melchizedek. And Moses.

He built up the nation of Israel into the Garden City of God—its Temple in Jerusalem, modeled after the Garden of Eden. Over Israel, he placed—you guessed it—prophets, priests, and kings.

All of them meant to show us exactly what we needed. Every priest was meant to show us that we needed a Great High Priest that could actually stand before God on our behalf. Every prophet showed us we needed not just a man to deliver God's word to us, but we needed the Prophet, the Word itself. Every king showed us we needed the one true King, the King of kings and the Lord of lords. That King would do the work Adam was designed to do—he would turn all of creation into the Garden City of God.

We needed God to do for us the work that only could be done by a man. Because no man could do it. No man was worthy. No man could overcome and undo what had been done. Earth could not climb its way back to heaven. But heaven could come down to earth.

Enter Jesus. God and man, two natures united in one person.

Jesus the Mediator

Jesus came to us as the King of heaven. He came to reclaim this world and establish his kingdom on earth. He came to establish himself as the King of kings and Lord of lords. He came as the eternal Word of God, to be our Prophet—God's living Word to us. He came as our Great High Priest, to live a perfect life and to sacrifice himself on our behalf, so that he could represent us before God.

As our Prophet, he reveals to us the Father and his law, and convicts us of our sin. As our Priest, he stands in God's presence on our behalf, bearing our sins while covering us in his own righteousness. As our King, he commands and empowers us to live holy lives in obedience to his word in every part of our lives.

He is the Mediator. The Savior. The Messiah. Paul, one of Jesus' apostles, wrote:

> He is the image of the invisible God, the firstborn of all creation. For by him all things were created, in heaven and on earth, visible and invisible, whether thrones or dominions or rulers or authorities—all things were created through him and for him. And he is before all things, and in him all things hold together. And he is the head of the body, the church. He is the beginning, the firstborn from the dead, that in everything he might be preeminent. For in him all the fullness of God was pleased to dwell,

and through him to reconcile to himself all things, whether on earth or in heaven, making peace by the blood of his cross.[3]

According to Ephesians 1:10, this was God's "plan for the fullness of time, to unite all things in him, things in heaven and things on earth."

So as our Savior—Jesus fulfills all three parts of what it means to be the Mediator between heaven and earth. He is the one true Prophet. He is the Great High Priest. And he is the King of kings and Lord of lords. He is the Savior of the world.

That's what the rest of this book is about.

3

The Final Word:
JESUS OUR PROPHET

Seeing the crowds, he went up on the mountain,
and when he sat down, his disciples came to him.
And he opened his mouth and taught them . . .

—Matthew 5:1–2

Not long ago, I was listening to someone tell a story about how their daughter loved music, but wasn't musical. They'd tried piano lessons and music lessons and all kinds of things to help her grow in her musicality—to no avail. Then this happened:

> About a year into her lessons, we were watching the movie *Happy Feet* about a penguin, Mumble, who has a big problem: He can't sing a single note, in a world where you need a heart song to attract a soul mate. Our daughter looked at me halfway through the movie and said, "Mom, am I like Mumble?"
>
> I was gripped in the moment by parental self-doubt. *What do I say? Do I tell her the truth and risk*

damaging her self-esteem, or do I lie and try to use the deception to kindle a love of music?

I took a risk. "Yes," I said, "you're pretty much like Mumble."

A big smile broke out across my daughter's face, which I interpreted as the smile of validation. I knew then I had done the right thing.[1]

Her daughter already knew the truth. Having it confirmed by her mother only validated her sense of self-awareness and gave her freedom to be herself—instead of pretending to be something she wasn't.

Contrast that to most parents today. Or schools. Or little leagues for that matter.

In the era of participation trophies and scoreless soccer games and graduation ceremonies *for every single grade*, it's easy to imagine the mom who answers, "Oh no, honey, I think you're very musical." Or to imagine the type of school that would respond to this little girl's *passion* for music with an award for musical excellence.

It's easy to imagine a scenario where, instead of being nurtured by the truth and encouraged to direct her passions elsewhere—this little girl is encouraged to embrace delusions about her own abilities. So that when she finally gets a music teacher that is honest with her—*I'm sorry, but perhaps you should try out for the soccer team*—she has no ability to distinguish the truth from the lie.

That's what a world full of flattery does to us.

It's not nice hearing that something you love and are passionate about just isn't a strength, no matter your level or age or what other strengths you possess. It's even harder to hear the truth—even if we suspect it really is true—when we've been flattered and lied to our entire lives.

But this is a problem not just in the world, but with the church across America.

Have you ever been to a church where it seemed like they just wanted you to feel good about yourself?

Or have you ever been to a church where you felt like nobody had any real problems? That everyone was expected to just smile and play nice? That if you ever went to the pastors or elders with real problems and sins, they wouldn't know what to do? That they might even be annoyed that you bothered them? That if you got real with them, you'd be breaking some kind of silent code, a conspiracy that runs along these lines: *Don't confess sin to us and we won't confront sin in you.*

That's true of churches in our day. And it was true of the religious leadership in the time of Jesus. God warns us about church leaders who flatter their people. He says they heal the wounds of his people lightly. Which, of course, isn't real healing. People don't need to be flattered. They need to hear the truth.

That's why Jesus came as our prophet.

The Ultimate Prophet

When you think of a prophet, what do you think of?

Someone who tells the future? Someone who has something special to say to you, specifically?

Here's the problem: those are pagan notions of what a prophet is. They've seeped in from oracles and soothsayers and fortune tellers. But that's not the main work of a prophet. Not in the Bible, anyway. That's just ancient paganism disguised as Christianity.

Do prophets in the Bible ever tell the future? They do. But, at the most basic level, a prophet is someone who reveals God's character and will. Someone who doesn't flatter people, but tells them the truth.

That's the work of a prophet. A prophet is a communicator. A teacher. Who reveals the character and will of God. (Which, at certain times, has involved revealing the future.)

The primary work of a prophet in Scripture is simple: to apply God's law to God's people.

In the Old Testament, the prophets would speak God's word on God's behalf. They'd reveal his will. They'd call out the sins of the people, and in particular, the sins of the kings and priests—the rulers and authorities. And when they did, they had a catchphrase: "Thus says the Lord."

They also performed signs and miracles that proved they were sent by God. Think of Moses and Elijah and Elisha, for example. Maybe you've read or heard some of their stories. They performed many miracles and signs that authenticated them as prophets sent by God to deliver the word of the LORD.

Moses parted the Red Sea and turned water into blood and a stick into a snake and warned Pharaoh of the plagues that were to come. Elijah and Elisha engaged with invisible armies, called fire down from heaven, healed lepers—even raised the dead. We don't have time or space to list it all, but the Old Testament is full of story after story of God sending someone to his people with a special message, and giving them authority and power to do miraculous deeds to prove they were from him.

Now, let's look at the life of Jesus.

Jesus was heralded by John the Baptist. He was baptized, and anointed Prophet, Priest, and King. He went into the wilderness and did battle with Satan, where he faced three temptations—the same ones Adam and Eve faced in the Garden—and conquered them all by quoting the word of God.

When he came out of his forty days of fasting and battle with Satan, he began to preach, saying, "Repent, for the kingdom of heaven is at hand."[2] In other words, the kingdom of heaven had now come down to earth. *It is here. And I am come to dethrone the god of this world and to take it all back.*

Then he went out through the synagogues, preaching and teaching and proclaiming the gospel of the kingdom to the poor and needy. Matthew 4 says he healed the sick and cast out demons. He was performing miracles greater than Moses or Elijah or Elisha.

And that brings us to the passage of Scripture I started this chapter with. Just as Moses climbed a mountain to receive God's law and give it to the people, Jesus went up on a mountain. But he didn't go visit with God and wait to receive his word. He sat down. And he opened his mouth. And he taught the people.

And when he spoke, he did not say, "Thus says the Lord." He said, "*I* tell you the truth." Or, "Truly, truly, *I* say to you."

He spoke as God.

Everywhere he went, the people were amazed. They said that no one ever spoke like this man. He had real authority. And he saved his hardest words for the leaders of the people, the false shepherds known as scribes and Pharisees. He called them "whitewashed tombs" and publicly accused them of being hypocrites, both to their faces and to anyone who would listen.

Why?

Jesus wasn't just a prophet. He was The Prophet. He didn't just proclaim God's word. He is God's eternal Word. He is the Word made flesh.

Everything that came before was just pictures—types and shadows.

Moses the prophet led God's people out of Egypt in the great exodus. There's a book of the Bible about it called—you guessed it—Exodus.

Remember Pharaoh? Take a minute and look up a picture of him. Do you think it's some coincidence of history that Pharaoh was the snake king of Egypt, with a headdress that made him look like a cobra, and with a serpent on his crown? Think about all that happened—the ten plagues, culminating in the death of the firstborn sons—except for those households that had the blood of a lamb over the door. Think of the parting of the Red Sea. Load as much of it up in your brain as you can going into this story:

In Luke 9, Jesus takes Peter and John and James up on a mountain to pray. And as Jesus was praying, his face was altered, and his clothes became a dazzling white. And two men appeared and were talking with him—Moses and Elijah.

James and John and Peter were asleep, but they woke up and saw what was going on. Peter was overwhelmed and excited and wanted to build tents for Moses and Elijah to stay in. And a voice came out of the cloud saying, "This is my Son, my Chosen One; listen to him!"

But, do you know what Jesus and Moses and Elijah were talking about? We actually know. It says. Your translation probably reads something like this, they "spoke of his departure, which he was about to accomplish at Jerusalem."[3]

Except, do you know what the Greek word for "departure" is? *Exodus.* They spoke of his *exodus*, which he was about to accomplish at Jerusalem.

Before he died, Moses spoke of a prophet that was to come. He told the people of Israel, "The Lord your God will raise up for you a prophet like me from among you, from your brothers—it is to him you shall listen."[4]

Jesus is that prophet. He came to lead us out of bondage and captivity to sin and Satan. He came to reveal the Father to us. To reveal the will of the Father to us. He is the first Word. And he is the last Word. The final Word.

Ever wonder why we don't have any more books of the Bible? Why we don't have any more continuing, ongoing revelation? We don't need them. Jesus is it.

Hebrews 1:1–3 says this:

Long ago, at many times and in many ways, God spoke to our fathers by the prophets, but in these last days he has spoken to us by his Son, whom he appointed the heir of all things, through whom also he created the world. He is the radiance of the glory of God and the exact imprint of his nature, and he upholds the universe by the word of his power.

The Prophetic Ministry of Jesus Today

Okay, so that's all big picture stuff. What does it mean for us today? Right now?

The prophetic ministry of Jesus has not stopped. It continues through the ministry of his word. Revealing to us God the Father, in all his holiness. And convicting us of our sin and our need for a Savior. Someone to stand in as our High Priest. A King to lead us.

But many churches today have lost the prophetic ministry of Jesus. They refuse to acknowledge it. Instead, they've turned to flattery and empty promises, like we talked about at the beginning of the chapter. They do this in a few ways.

1. Many churches replace preachers of the word with soothsayers and fortune tellers.

You know these churches. The preacher claims to have a special word from God. A new revelation that enables him to tell you how to get rich, or exactly when the world will end, or whatever. Lots of people make fun of these churches because they end up on TV or in the news—often when their predictions are wrong. Or made up just to take advantage of people.

The pastors and leaders of these churches really are just modern-day soothsayers and fortune tellers. With about the same success rate as any other soothsayer or fortune teller, reading bones and tea leaves.

They're often compromised at crucial places. Their new revelations from "God" are just a cover for their refusal to submit to God's actual revelations in the scriptures, through Jesus. Think about it. God's word says, "I do not permit a woman to teach or exercise authority over a man."⁵ Yet look at all the prophetesses around who know better, because they've received a word! Which is to say, they have a feeling deep inside that they should be allowed to disregard the clear teaching of God's word and do what they feel like.

They have elevated themselves above Jesus. And that makes them liars and charlatans. Not prophets.

2. Many churches focus on a cheap grace that loses the gospel call to obedience.

Prophets call for obedience. Especially at the hardest places. Think of Jesus and his Sermon on the Mount. Sex, Anger, Money, Divorce, Idolatry, Worry, Revenge, Self-Righteousness, Hypocrisy, Prayer, Generosity, Heaven and Hell, and *more*—all dealt with in *the same sermon.*

By contrast, there are churches you can go to where you will never hear a sermon on any one of those topics.

You'll hear words like "grace" and "forgiveness," maybe. But no calls to obedience. And with that, no promise of power to change. Which makes the grace of God and the forgiveness we have in Jesus cheap.

Grace is free, but it is never cheap. And God's grace comes to us, never just as forgiveness, but as power to change and walk in obedience to God's commands.

3. Many churches end up healing wounds lightly when sin is real and hard and unavoidable.

You have real sin. Real weight. You feel it. And this is the response you get:

It's okay, Jesus has already forgiven you, you don't need to feel guilt or shame. You don't need to repent.
BUT I FEEL BAD.
That's your sin. You don't believe in grace.
BUT I WANT TO CHANGE.
You're focused on works. What you need is grace.

This is what false shepherds do. Is your conscience afflicted? They have nothing for you. Except cheap, superficial healing. (Usually this is because they have their own horrible sin they would have to deal with before they were ever able to truly deal with yours.)

This was why Jesus' ministry was so powerful. Because we all know that everything is not okay. We all know we have sin. It goes deep down. Jesus only told the people what we all already know.

Sin is real. God is holy.

Your anger? It's wrong. It's murder. Jesus said so.

Your lust? It's wrong. God is holy. Jesus said so.

What a relief! Just to be told: That thing in your heart? That makes you feel guilty? You *should* feel guilty. God agrees with you and condemns that sin. There's hope in that.

Why?

Because if God sent someone to tell us about our sin, that must mean it's not too late. It must mean there's more to the story. Otherwise, why would he bother?

Ultimately, if you listen to the liars, their real message is that there is no hope. There is no power. You're stuck in your sin. Sort of like the girl at the beginning of this chapter, stuck trying to be musical forever, because nobody dared tell her she lacked the talent.

Sin is a lot worse than a lack of talent. It's a horrible problem that you *must* deal with. If someone lies to you about that, or heals it falsely, what can you do but despair?

But Jesus is a prophet. Jesus is The Prophet. And a prophet who is hope itself. When you're reading Scripture, when you're sitting under the preaching of the word, and it afflicts your conscience, you can trust it.

Because Jesus is a prophet who afflicts us, so that he can heal us. Because he is a prophet who is not just a prophet. He is a prophet who is also a priest. And that means forgiveness. And he is a prophet who is also a king. And that means power to change.

4

Blood-Bought:

JESUS OUR PRIEST

So they took Jesus, and he went out, bearing his own cross, to the place called The Place of a Skull, which in Aramaic is called Golgotha. There they crucified him, and with him two others, one on either side, and Jesus between them.

—John 19:16–18

If a prophet's job is to confront us with the truth, revealing to us God's character and will, and Jesus is the Prophet who did that perfectly, that leaves us with a problem.

We can't measure up to God's holiness. We've failed to live according to his will, in perfect obedience. And that means we fall short. We stand guilty.

We all know this deep down, and that's why it can be a relief to just hear it said to us, plainly and clearly.

But the simple fact is, most of us spend our lives living in denial about just how bad we really are, and just how deep our sinfulness goes.

Alone on our beds at night, we contemplate our failures and our mistakes. That's why many people medicate themselves with alcohol or sedatives every evening. The mistakes and sins and failures are overwhelming and we want to forget.

It's also why we fill up our lives with distractions. It's scary to be alone with our own thoughts. So from the moment we wake up in the morning, until we go to bed at night, we fill every second of our lives with noise. This is one place modern technology has been more of a hindrance than a help to many.

Smartphones, social media, on-demand streaming services for music, podcasts, TV, movies, and more, all trigger our dopamine receptors, steal away our moments of self-reflection, and leave us a little more numb.

As much as we'd like to suppress the truth about God and ourselves, it does have its way of working itself out though. Have you ever considered the purpose of the horror genre, for instance?

For most of a standard horror movie, a nameless, faceless primordial power of some sort threatens to overwhelm the characters that stand in for us. We watch as vengeance is enacted, often as retribution for sins, on helpless victims. And ultimately, when the sacrifices are complete, things resume as normal.

We walk out of movie theaters feeling some sense of cathartic release. We've dealt with our sins. For a time.

These cinematic sacrifices really aren't that different from the ritual sacrifices pervasive across all cultures. The main difference is that they're simulated and mediated through a screen, with our artists and filmmakers serving as our priests.

You may have never thought about it quite like that. But I bet when you hear the word "priest," you think of sacrifice.

Sacrifice

Sacrifice runs deep and finds its way into every culture on the planet, because sin and its guilt run deep. And the sense that sin must be atoned for—that it requires sacrifice, death, blood—runs deep.

After Adam and Eve fell in the Garden of Eden and God pronounced his curses—and also the promise that the seed of the woman would crush the head of the snake—God made clothes for Adam and Eve. Not out of fig leaves—the cheap covering they made for themselves—but out of animal skins. The first sacrifice.

Cain and Abel made sacrifices to God.

Noah made sacrifices.

Melchizedek, Job, Abraham, Isaac, Jacob—all made sacrifices to God.

Through Moses, God established a priesthood whose job was to make sacrifices. The highest occasion for sacrifice in the Old Testament was the Day of Atonement.

This day was the one day out of the year where a

priest, one priest, the High Priest, was allowed into the Holy of Holies, the center of the Temple, the Most Holy Place, where God's presence dwelt above the Ark of the Covenant. It was terrifying. Because God is holy.

To offer the sacrifices, the High Priest first had to sacrifice a bull for his own sins so that he could come into God's presence to sacrifice on behalf of the people.

Then he offered two goats. One goat was the sin offering for the people. It bore the wrath of sin. There's a word for that, it's called propitiation.

Then there was another goat, called the scapegoat. The priest would lay his hands on the goat and pronounce the sins of the people. Then that goat would be sent out into the wilderness to remove the guilt of sin from the presence of God and his people. There's a word for that, it's called expiation. The removal of sin.

Together these would atone for the sins of the people.

Except the blood of bulls and goats could never atone for sin. They were only ritual. They were symbolic. They only taught the people of the need for atonement. They reinforced that innate need for a sacrifice. But animals could not accomplish the work they represented.

Man sinned. Man needed to die.

The pagans understood this. That's why human sacrifice is interwoven into human history. In fact, all murder is, in some sense, human sacrifice. Sacrifices are made to appease the gods and get something.

James tells us, "You desire and do not have, so you murder."[1] We don't get what we want from God, so we attack the image of God in man.

Cain was angry. His sacrifice wasn't accepted. So he sacrificed his brother.

God promised that the seed, the child of the woman, would crush the head of the snake. What sacrifice has the snake always demanded? Children.

Pharaoh, the snake king, demanded the sacrifice of the Hebrew children when Moses arose.

Herod, threatened by the birth of Jesus, demanded the sacrifice of the children of Bethlehem.

Molech, that pagan demon god, has always demanded the sacrifice of children in exchange for a bountiful harvest and economic prosperity. And pagans have always obeyed.

Abortion is the pagan sacrifice of our children for a bountiful harvest and economic prosperity. We hide it. We cover it up. We act like we're not religious. But instead of our streets running with the blood of bulls and goats, our sewers run with the blood of our children.

The farther we move from Jesus as a culture, the more we just become ancient pagans. And like the ancient pagans, we pair our sacrifice of children with sexual debauchery.

None of it is sufficient. Molech cannot be appeased by children. And the living God cannot be appeased by bulls and goats.

Our High Priest

Enter Jesus. Our Great High Priest.

Jesus, because of his perfect obedience to God the Father, because of his perfection as God himself made flesh, is worthy to stand in God's presence on our behalf. He doesn't have to offer any sacrifice for himself. His obedience stands in place of our obedience.

And he made full and complete sacrifice of the only life sufficient to remove our guilt. His own. He bore God's wrath on our behalf (propitiation). And he removed sin (expiation). He atoned for our sins through his death on a cross.

Adam ate the fruit of the tree and fell.

Jesus climbed the tree—the cross—and laid down his life. He ate the fruit of Adam's fall. He tasted death.

Adam gave his crown to Satan and the curse of sin and death entered the world.

Jesus bore the curse in his own body, wearing a crown of thorns.

All of this is summed up by the prophet Isaiah, writing hundreds of years before the birth of Jesus:

> Surely our griefs He Himself bore,
> And our sorrows He carried;
> Yet we ourselves esteemed Him stricken,
> Smitten of God, and afflicted.
> But He was pierced through for our
> transgressions,

He was crushed for our iniquities;
The chastening for our well-being fell upon
	Him,
And by His scourging we are healed.
All of us like sheep have gone astray,
Each of us has turned to his own way;
But the LORD has caused the iniquity of us all
To fall on Him.

He was oppressed and He was afflicted,
Yet He did not open His mouth;
Like a lamb that is led to slaughter,
And like a sheep that is silent before its shearers,
So He did not open His mouth.

. . .

But the LORD was pleased
To crush Him, putting Him to grief;
If He would render Himself as a guilt offering,
He will see His offspring,
He will prolong His days,
And the good pleasure of the LORD will
	prosper in His hand.
As a result of the anguish of His soul,
He will see it and be satisfied;
By His knowledge the Righteous One,
My Servant, will justify the many,
As He will bear their iniquities.
Therefore, I will allot Him a portion with the
	great,

> And He will divide the booty with the strong;
> Because He poured out Himself to death,
> And was numbered with the transgressors;
> Yet He Himself bore the sin of many,
> And interceded for the transgressors.[2]

He has done it. It is finished. Jesus is our High Priest. And he stands today as our High Priest, between God and us. When God looks at the believer, God sees the perfect righteousness of Christ. And he does not remember our sins. As far as the east is from the west, so far has he removed our sins from us.

There's no sacrifice for us to offer. There's no penance to complete. Jesus has done it. What we could never do. He traded his perfect life for our lives of sin. And his reward for our punishment.

Come to Christ

So come to him. Bring your guilt and your shame. Bring your sin. In all of its ugliness. Don't be afraid to admit it. To confess it. To own it. You have rung bells that can't be unrung. Lay them at the foot of the cross.

Come to the tree. Admit that you are like Adam and Eve. You ate the fruit. And you cannot bear the weight.

And leave your life there. He gave his life for yours. All of him for all of you. Now live your life for him. All of you for all of him. For all the world. Starting at home. With your husband or wife and kids and brothers and sisters and mom and dad. And with your church family. And with your neighbors. And coworkers. And with your community.

5

Taking It All Back:
JESUS OUR KING

The angel said to the women, "Do not be afraid, for I know that you seek Jesus who was crucified. He is not here, for he has risen, as he said. Come, see the place where he lay. Then go quickly and tell his disciples that he has risen from the dead, and behold, he is going before you to Galilee; there you will see him. See, I have told you."

—Matthew 28:5–7

Not long ago I sat down with my family and watched *The Sound of Music.* These days, we don't really sit down to watch movies more than maybe once a month or so, because baseball, soccer, fun outside, etc. But yesterday it turned cold and rainy. And my oldest son had to go to the hospital and get stitches and was down. And I was on edge, because I often get on edge as we get closer to Sunday morning and my sermon prep isn't done.

And so I just wanted comfort food. And when it comes to movies, some comfort food is more wholesome than others, more for the whole family than others. And that's what I wanted.

I picked *The Sound of Music*—one of my favorite

69

things—so (a needle pulling thread) I could relax, follow along with the beats, work on my sermon in peace, while Amanda made dinner and took care of whatever else she had to take care of.

I don't know . . . I suppose it's not especially manly to admit that you love *The Sound of Music*. I suppose it's even worse to admit that you cry pretty much every time you watch it. But I do. I *always* do. And it's not just the story of the beautiful woman who softens the heart of the grieving widower and father that gets to me.

Yes, that's part of it. But it's also that this ordinary, prosaic story about a motherless family with an overbearing father is set in the midst of such turmoil and chaos.

And it always draws my heart and my mind to reflect on the turmoil and chaos of the changing times we live in. It makes me mourn for the ways our country has changed and is changing—for the America I grew up in. It awakens this sense, that, no matter how hard I try, I can't quite give that to my kids.

And that has to be okay. I have to be okay with that. With God's help, and only with God's help, I can give them something more—a father who has the moral courage to stand firm in the midst of a trying and difficult time.

That's the way *The Sound of Music* always hits me. And I knew that when I turned it on. And it hit me that way anyway.

And I'm bringing it up at the top of this chapter,

because we live in a time of turmoil. Things are shifting around us constantly. The world we live in today is different than the world of a year ago. And two years ago. And in some ways, ten years ago is already unrecognizable.

Kingdoms come and go. Empires rise and fall. All nations are a drop in the bucket. There's nothing extraordinary about an empire rising to prominence, getting decadent, growing murderous and sexually perverse, and eating itself alive as it falls into decay and ruin.

I'm not trying to be a prophet of doom and gloom for America. I'm just saying, that's the way things tend to go. And if we hope to have anything to say about it, we have to be honest in our assessment of where we're at.

So I'm thinking these sorts of thoughts, and I'm sad. I'm trying to work on a sermon. And that sermon is what became this chapter. And it is the answer to this sadness. It is the hope and the strength and the power we need to face whatever comes with absolute confidence and courage and strength.

Because Jesus is King. Our King.

So if you feel what I feel, if inflation is hitting your wallet and bank account and making you sweat, if the prospect of food shortages and monkey viruses and riots hits you where you live, this chapter is for you.

This is the fifth and final chapter in our study of the person and work of Jesus. And it ends where our story ends. Victory over sin and death and hell. The triumph of our King.

Let's recap very quickly. Who is Jesus?

Jesus is God. The eternal God. Everything was made by him and through him. He is God. From eternity past—before any of us were, he is.

This changes everything. It changes how we look at and understand the Bible and the world and ourselves in the world and how we live and the whole scope of human history. All of it. Jesus is God, and that changes everything.

Before, we thought the solar system revolved around the earth. Now we know that our world revolves around the sun. That's how revolutionary it is. If we don't know Jesus, we think everything revolves around us. But Jesus is God. So no. It revolves around him.

Jesus is God. Jesus became man. He lived for nine months in the womb of a girl named Mary. Then he was born. He lived just like us. He was hungry and thirsty and tired, he ate and slept and drank. He grew up. He hit puberty. He worked with his hands. He experienced the full range of human emotions—he got angry, he got sad, he cried. And he was tempted in every way as we are, yet without sin.

And that means, because he is like us in every way, he understands us in every way. And not just in a sovereign, God-understands-everything sort of way. He walked it himself. He lived it himself. There is nothing you've ever been through, nothing you're going through, nothing you will go through, that he can't relate to. Which means we have a God that we can come to who understands us perfectly.

And Jesus is our Mediator. He stands between heaven and earth, between God and all of creation, between God and man.

Jesus lived a life where he preached to us. He taught us who God the Father is and what God the Father expects of us. He showed us the character of God in his actions. He proved everything he had to say with signs and wonders and miracles. He put the liars and false shepherds and hypocrites in their place. He called sinners like us to repent and turn to him. And when he did that he gave us hope. Because he told us all the truth. And he called us to return to God. Jesus is our prophet. He came to us from heaven with a message. And he delivered that message perfectly.

Then Jesus, having lived a perfect life, laid down his life. He sacrificed himself on our behalf. Adam, our first father, ate the forbidden fruit of the tree and inherited a curse of sin and death that he passed down to us. Jesus climbed up on a tree with a crown of thorns on his head, and he suffered the full curse of sin and death on our behalf. He bore our sins in his body on the tree. He bore our curse—the curse of sin and death and hell. He who knew no sin became sin on our behalf, so that in him we might become the righteousness of God.

He did this so that he could stand before God the Father as our Great High Priest. His sacrifice atones for our sins. His righteous life stands in our place. He stands between us and God in such a way that when God looks at us, he sees Jesus. Jesus is our priest.

But what happened next?

They took him. They buried him in a tomb. They sealed it. And three days later, he stood up, folded his grave clothes, and walked away.

He won. He didn't just bear the punishment of our sins. He destroyed them. He didn't just die. He killed death. From that point on, the world has worked backwards. Life from death. Beauty from ashes.

This is the triumph of our King. He unseated the devil. Adam gave Satan his crown in the Garden. Jesus climbed the cross, he bore the curse, and he took it back. And his resurrection is the ultimate proof that he won.

> He himself likewise partook of the same things [flesh and blood], that through death he might destroy the one who has the power of death, that is, the devil, and deliver all those who through fear of death were subject to lifelong slavery.[1]

He took it all back. And then he just walked around for a little bit and told his disciples, I told you so. And ate some fish and got them ready for the work he was about to have them do.

Because they had work to do. And that's why we're here. We are their work. And our job is to continue that work. What work? Here it is:

And Jesus came and said to them, "All authority in heaven and on earth has been given to me. Go therefore and make disciples of all nations, baptizing them in the name of the Father and of the Son and of the Holy Spirit, teaching them to observe all that I have commanded you. And behold, I am with you always, to the end of the age."[2]

Let's break that down:

All Authority Belongs to Jesus

What does that mean? Exactly what we've been saying all along.

God made Adam a king. And Adam, as king, gave his authority to Satan in the Garden.

This is why Scripture calls Satan in one place "the god of this world."[3] Or speaks of the demonic principalities and powers of this world.[4]

Jesus came and took it all back. Single-handedly. It was always his anyway. But now there is no question. And sin, death, the devil—they have no claim. Because Jesus is alive.

Therefore God has highly exalted him and bestowed

on him the name that is above every name, so that at the name of Jesus every knee should bow, in heaven and on earth and under the earth, and every tongue confess that Jesus Christ is Lord, to the glory of God the Father.[5]

Up until that point, God's people had only laid claim to a small amount of territory in this world. God was only worshiped by a family of people descended from a man named Abraham. He had been working in and through that family for thousands of years.

But now that Jesus had come and won the decisive victory, it was time to engage in worldwide conquest.

Jesus stepped forward from the grave and said to his disciples, *All authority in heaven and on earth is mine. Therefore, Go. Make disciples of all nations. Baptize them in the name of the Father, Son, and Holy Spirit. And teach them to obey everything I've commanded you. I will be with you to the end.*

And so here it is. Jesus has all authority. No one can cross him now. No one can stand up to him. He has won. And he has told us to go and conquer the nations. To exercise his dominion in all the earth.

How?

Not with a sword of steel. But with the sword of the Spirit. With his word. Eleven men stood on a mountain and heard this command: *Go and make disciples of all nations. Baptize them and teach them to obey everything. I'm with you.*

And they went. And then Jesus ascended into heaven and sat down at the right hand of God the Father Almighty:

> When Christ had offered for all time a single sacrifice for sins, he sat down at the right hand of God, waiting from that time until his enemies should be made a footstool for his feet.[6]

This is how the Apostle Peter put it on the day of Pentecost in Acts 2:

> This Jesus God raised up, and of that we all are witnesses. Being therefore exalted at the right hand of God, and having received from the Father the promise of the Holy Spirit, he has poured out this that you yourselves are seeing and hearing. For David did not ascend into the heavens, but he himself says, "The Lord said to my Lord, 'Sit at my right hand, until I make your enemies your footstool.'"[7]

In Ephesians 1, the Apostle Paul is praying for the church at Ephesus, that they may know the hope they are called to and the power at work in them, and this is how he describes that power and might:

> . . . according to the working of his great might that he worked in Christ when he raised him from the dead and seated him at his right hand in the

heavenly places, far above all rule and authority and power and dominion and above every name that is named, not only in this age but also in the one to come. And he put all things under his feet and gave him as head over all things to the church.[8]

There are more passages like that we could read. But did you notice a funny little thread in there?

Something about feet.

Here's the deal. Jesus is right now reigning as King of kings and Lord of lords over heaven and earth. He has already won the decisive victory. It is over. It's all his. And now our job, as his church, is to go into all the world and declare his victory, and take it all back for him. To realize that victory.

The Bible has three ways of talking about our salvation.

The first is past tense. You were saved. That's being free from the guilt of sin. That's called justification. And that happens as soon as we believe in Jesus.

The second is present tense. You are being saved. And that's being free from the power of sin. That's called sanctification. And that's our whole life's work.

The third is future tense. You will be saved. And that's being free from the presence of sin. And that's called glorification. And that's what happens when we die or when Jesus returns.

The Bible also has three ways of talking about Jesus' victory.

Through his death and resurrection, Jesus has won. Objectively. Past tense. He's the King.

Jesus ascended into heaven and sat down at the right hand of the Father. That's where he is today. Jesus is King, present tense. Jesus is winning. Just like we, as believers, spend our lives subduing our own sins and submitting ourselves to our King—resolving to walk in his ways in obedience to his commands. Our job is to see his kingdom come and his will be done on earth as it is in heaven. To build his kingdom here and now.

One day, Jesus will win. His victory will be complete, future tense. And he will return to judge the living and the dead. And make all things right. Victory sealed.

Now What?

So what does this mean for you?

It means that Jesus is your King. And that means you have nothing to be afraid of. Jesus fought your fight. He faced down every one of your sins. Even the ones you have a hard time facing. He took them on his own shoulders.

He said, *Your sins are now mine, your burdens, mine, your problems, mine.* And then he beat them all. He bore their guilt and punishment. And he died. And then he got back up again.

He fought the fight you could never fight. The fight

you could never win. The fight you deserved to lose. And he won.

And now he's your King. And your job is to submit to him in every part of your life. To be baptized and to obey everything that he has commanded.

And because Jesus is your King, you also don't have to worry about anyone *out there*. You don't have to worry about Washington, D.C. You don't have to worry about your enemies.

Jesus is placing all his enemies under his feet. They can't stand against him. They will bow down or they will break.

Because Jesus is King, you don't have to worry about the progress of the gospel. Because it cannot be stopped. In fact, you can work fearlessly to build and spread God's kingdom. To make disciples of all nations. To teach them to obey everything Jesus commanded. Starting with your family. With your kids. With your neighbors and friends.

Why?

Because Jesus has already won. And Jesus is winning. And Jesus will win. And one way or another, every knee will bow.

Jesus wins. So we win. So long as we remain faithful to him.

Jesus is King everywhere. There's not one square inch in all of creation that he does not reign over as King. And we—you and I—get to be part of that. We get to be at this grand little outpost known as our local church. For me, it's Church of the King in Evansville, Indiana.

And the fact that we're here doing this very work is 100% proof positive that Jesus is the risen King and has been reigning as the risen King for over two thousand years, and that he cares about this square inch of dirt too. He wants it all. And he will have it all.

So have faith for that. And have faith for it all the time.

Royal Ambassadors:
LIVING FOR THE KING

Whom shall I send? And who will go for us?

—Isaiah 6:8

When Amanda and I moved to the Evansville area, we bought new construction. It was a huge step for us. We'd lived in this house built in the '60s that had all kinds of problems, and it served us well. But I didn't want to move down here and have house work and projects and things falling apart and unforeseen expenses while trying to plant a church in the summer of 2020. So we bought new construction.

One Friday morning in April, not long after we moved, I noticed that the thermostat was set to 68 and the temperature in the house was 74. So I went to work. I did all the things. I changed the filter, I checked the breakers, I took the panel off the back of my AC unit to examine the state of the capacitor.

And after some effort, I figured out the capacitor was shot.

Thanks to help from a long-time friend in HVAC, I knew that I could replace it myself. But I also knew that in order to do that, I'd have to order the capacitor and wait for it to ship. At this point in the day, the temperature was already in the 90s, and the rest of the week wasn't looking better. I was also angry and frustrated, because this was exactly the type of problem we were trying to avoid when we bought new construction. And then it dawned on me . . . *Hey, this house is new construction. It wasn't built in the '60s. I bet this AC unit and the work is all under warranty. You actually don't have to figure this out yourself.*

So I made a couple calls, and within an hour or so, the HVAC guy showed up at my house, and I told him what was up and he fixed it fast—because I had already done the diagnostic work and prepped it all.

Then, even though parts and labor were free, he charged me $60 for diagnosing a problem I had already diagnosed.

As you can imagine, I found this all very annoying. The hassle. The time out of my day. The work I put into figuring it all out, only to still have to pay a stupid diagnostic fee. And I get it, gas isn't cheap and people need to be paid, but that doesn't mean I have to be happy about it, right?

Then it started to happen.

The HVAC technician started asking me what I do for a living. Yikes. Here I am, hot, angry, tired, annoyed at his very existence, and I have to tell him that . . . I'm a pastor. But I told him and we got to talking, just the same.

Over the course of our conversation, I learned that this man is a believer, but he hadn't been to church faithfully since Covid lockdowns. And I learned that he had a bad conscience about it.

What's more, as we kept talking, I learned that he had deep ties to many people in our church—family connections, childhood friendships, and more.

So, guess what finally occurred to me? What finally got through my thick skull?

Maybe the reason my air conditioning broke down is because God means to call this man back to himself.

And then he promised to come to church, and who knows how it will end?

Jesus does. Because Jesus planned it from the beginning.

Jesus is King. And we all have people that God brings into our lives all the time. We need to always believe that God brings people into our lives because he means to save them. Because he means to make them his disciples too.

Remember, every knee will bow before the King. Our goal is to see as many people bow in this life, before they have to face him in judgment.

So do it. Find a church that lives and believes

it—that worships and serves the King and that exercises his dominion in the world.

And then become like Jesus. Be what you were made to be from the beginning—in Christ all things are restored. Go and be prophets—speak truth into every part of the world you live in. Be priests—reconcile people to God through the blood of our Great High Priest. Be kings—and see his kingdom expand and fill the earth, starting with your home, your children, your neighborhood, your community, your city.

Submit your life—all of it—to the King. And live to see his kingdom come, and his will be done, on earth as it is in heaven.

Wait a second. Record scratch. That all sounds great, but if you really are new to this stuff, you're going to need more than that. How do you practically begin to obey and become like Jesus?

Well . . . whole books have been written on that topic. Sixty-six books of the Bible, in fact. And countless others. As in, literally, we couldn't count them if we wanted to.

So read your Bible. That's a good starting place. And pray that God would help you understand it. Pray and approach it with humility. The Bible is clear, yes. But that doesn't mean everybody comes to a correct understanding of every passage the first time they read it. Actually, nobody does.

Which is why you need help. You can't do it by yourself. Your primary help will be from Jesus, working through the Holy Spirit in your life. But there's a specific way that God works on us, and that's his church. After all, Jesus' kingdom is bigger than you. It's bigger than me. He didn't come to the earth just to save this or that person, but to save a *people*, a *holy nation* for himself.[1]

So I'll say it again: Find a church that worships and serves the King. You need a church that believes in the whole Bible as the inspired Word of God. A church that won't flatter you, but will tell you the truth. About Jesus, about God's law, about yourself. Give yourself to the church. Go on Sunday mornings. If the doors are open, if people are gathering, be there. Meet people. Get to know the pastors. Find ways to serve. Find ways to grow.

That's the best and most practical step for beginning to submit your life to the King.

NOTES

Part One. Who Do You Say I Am?

1. Isaiah 9:1 (ESV, NIV).

2. Matthew 16:15.

1. Jesus Is God

1. Mark 8:27.

2. Matthew 16:14.

3. Matthew 16:15.

4. Matthew 16:16.

5. Matthew 16:17. "Bar-Jonah" means "son of Jonah."

6. C. S. Lewis, *Mere Christianity* (1952, 1980; HarperCollins, 2001), 52.

7. Psalm 66:3 (NASB 1995).

8. John 1:1–4.

9. Colossians 1:15.

10. John 1:18.

11. Genesis 3:8.

12. Genesis 7:16.

13. Genesis 32:24–30.

14. Exodus 3:2.

15. Daniel 3:24–25.

16. Isaiah 6:1–3.

2. Jesus Is Man

1. Revelation 19:15–16.

2. Mark 6:3.

3. John 11:3.

4. Mark 10:14.

5. Mark 3:4.

6. Mark 3:5.

7. Matthew 23:24.

8. Matthew 7:3–5.

9. John 7:5 (NASB 1995).

10. See Matthew 4:3.

11. Charles Spurgeon, "Jesus Wept," sermon preached at Metropolitan Tabernacle on June 23, 1889, https://www.spurgeon.org/resource-library/sermons/jesus-wept/.

Part Two. Jesus Our Mediator

1. Genesis 2:7.

2. 2 Corinthians 4:4.

3. Colossians 1:15–20.

3. Jesus Our Prophet

1. Anna Lembke, *Dopamine Nation: Finding Balance in the Age of Indulgence* (Dutton, 2021), ch. 9. Italics original.

2. Matthew 4:17.

3. Luke 9:31.

4. Deuteronomy 18:15.

5. 1 Timothy 2:12.

4. Jesus Our Priest

1. James 4:2.

2. Isaiah 53:4–7, 10–12 (NASB 1995).

5. Jesus Our King

1. Hebrews 2:14–15.
2. Matthew 28:18–20
3. 2 Corinthians 4:4.
4. See Ephesians 6:12.
5. Philippians 2:9–11.
6. Hebrews 10:12–13.
7. Acts 2:32–35.
8. Ephesians 1:19–22.

Conclusion. Living for the King

1. 1 Peter 2:9.

www.ingramcontent.com/pod-product-compliance
Lightning Source LLC
Chambersburg PA
CBHW061033050726
47592CB00004B/1422